THE CHILD NO ONE STOPPED

The True Crime Story of Damari Carter

Linda Davidson

Copyright © 2025 Linda Davidson

All rights reserved

No part of this book may be reproduced, or stored in a retrieval system, or transmitted in any form or by any means, electronic, mechanical, photocopying, recording, or otherwise, without express written permission of the publisher.

*For the children who needed protection— and
for the people who chose to notice.*

"Rescue those being led away to death; hold back those staggering toward slaughter."

—PROVERBS 24:11

CONTENTS

Title Page
Copyright
Dedication
Epigraph
Prologue
Preface

Chapter 1 The Discovery	1
Chapter 2 What They Could Say	4
Chapter 3 A Child Without a Name	7
Chapter 4 Someone Had Seen Him	10
Chapter 5 A Home That Looked Normal	13
Chapter 7 The Last Time He Was Seen	16
Chapter 8 Reports That Went Nowhere	19
Chapter 9 Red Flags	22
Chapter 10 The Visit That Changed Nothing	25
Chapter 11 How Abuse Hid	28
Chapter 12 The Final Days	31
Chapter 13 The Moment It Ended	34
Chapter 14 The Investigation Shifts	37
Chapter 15 Accountability	40
Chapter 16 The Child No One Stopped	43

Epilogue	47
Also in the Series	49
A Personal Request	51
Next in The Series…	53
Also by Linda Davidson	55
About the Author	57
If You are Worried About a Child	59
Content Note	61
Author's Message to the Reader	63
Acknowledgement	65
Author's Note	67
Disclaimer	69
Sources and Research Notes	71
References	73

PROLOGUE

— The Bag

It was early enough that the day hadn't decided what it would be yet.

Garbage trucks moved through the street on their usual route. A few doors opened and closed. Someone paused longer than normal near the curb, noticing something that hadn't been there the day before—or maybe had, just not long enough to register.

A bag.

Not new. Not torn apart. Just out of place.

At first glance, it didn't demand attention. Bags get left behind all the time. People move things, abandon things, forget things. The street had seen worse and shrugged it off before.

But there was something about the way it sat—positioned, not tossed. Closed, not spilling. Present in a way that felt deliberate.

The call that followed was cautious. Measured. No raised voice. No urgency. The kind of report that begins with uncertainty rather than alarm. A description offered carefully, as if the caller didn't want to sound foolish for noticing something ordinary.

Dispatch logged it. Officers were sent.

When they arrived, they didn't rush.

They approached the bag the way people do when they don't yet know they're standing at the edge of something irreversible. From the outside, there was nothing dramatic to see. No blood. No smell that forced an immediate conclusion. No sign that whatever was inside demanded speed instead of procedure.

Still, there was a pause.

A moment where routine slowed.

The bag was photographed where it sat. Notes were taken. Radio traffic stayed neutral, clipped, professional. The language was careful—noncommittal, almost bland. Words that left room for anything and nothing at the same time.

When the bag was finally opened, no one spoke right away.

The silence that followed wasn't shock in the cinematic sense. It was recognition—quiet and immediate. The kind that doesn't need explanation because it rearranges everything the moment it lands.

What was found inside did not become public information right away.

It was described later in the vaguest possible terms. A body. A child. An investigation underway. More details to come.

But from the moment the bag was opened, the direction of the day changed. What had started as an ordinary morning narrowed into something smaller and heavier, something that would pull in investigators, reporters, and eventually an entire city searching for answers that wouldn't come cleanly.

The bag was removed. The street reopened. Life resumed its rhythm.

But something had already broken.

Because before the discovery, the child inside the bag had existed somewhere—inside a home, inside routines, inside a world that had room for adults and systems and safeguards.

And yet, the first undeniable moment anyone stopped came here.

On the street.

With a bag.

Too late.

The story did not begin with this discovery.

But this is where it could no longer be ignored.

PREFACE

Some cases arrive with noise.

Sirens. Breaking alerts. A rush of certainty that tells the public exactly what to feel before anyone has had time to understand what happened.

This story does not begin that way.

It begins with something that looked ordinary—an object out of place, a moment of hesitation, a call made carefully because the caller wasn't sure it mattered. And that is part of what makes this case so hard to sit with. Not the spectacle of violence, but the quietness of how the world can keep moving while a child is slipping out of view.

The Child No One Stopped is the true crime story of Damari Carter. It is also, unavoidably, a story about what society often labels as "everyday": strained homes, fragmented systems, delayed responses, and warning signs that never rise high enough to trigger the kind of action that saves a life. In cases like this, the tragedy doesn't always hinge on one moment. It builds through many—each small enough to explain away, each familiar enough to normalize, until there is a point where the only undeniable moment left is the one that comes too late.

This book was written to hold two truths at once.

The first is that Damari was a child—more than a headline, more than a case number, more than the final place he was found.

He was a living person who deserved protection before he ever needed justice.

The second is that this case asks difficult questions that do not end at the courtroom door. When a child's life becomes invisible, it is rarely because no one was nearby. More often, it's because concern never gathered enough momentum to become intervention—because responsibility is shared until it feels like it belongs to no one.

You will not find shock for shock's sake in these pages. You will find procedure, chronology, and the slow work of truth: how investigators build a case from fragments, how institutions document without connecting, how silence becomes a kind of shelter for harm. You will also find what matters most: remembrance that refuses to reduce a child to evidence.

If you continue, I ask only this—read with care. Not just for the details, but for what they reveal about how easily ordinary life can hide extraordinary danger, and how much power there is in one person choosing to notice before a story reaches its ending.

Because the most devastating question in this case is also the simplest:

What if someone had stopped it sooner.

CHAPTER 1 THE DISCOVERY

The discovery did not arrive with chaos.

It arrived with procedure. Officers approached the scene with the calm that comes from routine calls. The kind where nothing has yet declared itself urgent. The bag sat where it had been reported —closed, intact, unremarkable in appearance.

They followed protocol. Secured the immediate area. Noted surroundings. Spoke briefly with the person who had called it in. The questions were standard. The answers were uncertain.

No one used the word *emergency*.

Not yet.

From the outside, there was little to observe.

The bag showed no obvious damage. It hadn't been ripped open or disturbed. It appeared intentionally placed rather than discarded in haste. There were no visible signs that would force an immediate conclusion.

But observation is not only visual.

Something about the situation resisted easy explanation. The bag didn't belong there. And while that alone isn't a crime, it was enough to slow the process—to introduce hesitation where there usually isn't any.

That hesitation mattered.

In the earliest moments, no one knew which questions would matter most.

No one could yet ask where the bag had come from, how long it had been there, or who might have noticed it earlier and thought nothing of it. Those questions come later, once the significance is clear.

At the time, the focus was narrow. Immediate. Procedural.

The larger questions waited quietly.

At first, there was room for ordinary explanations.

Abandoned property. Misplaced belongings. A routine issue that would be resolved without consequence. These assumptions are not careless—they're human. They are how people move through daily life without constant alarm.

But assumptions shape response.

And early assumptions, once formed, can delay recognition of what doesn't fit.

By the time certainty replaced uncertainty, the moment for interruption had already passed.

Whatever had led to the bag being placed there had happened elsewhere, earlier, without witnesses or intervention. The discovery could reveal what was done—but it could not undo what had already been allowed to unfold.

What stood before investigators was not the beginning of a crime.

It was the end of a long silence.

And from that point forward, every step would be about understanding how a child could reach this moment without being stopped sooner.

CHAPTER 2 WHAT THEY COULD SAY

The first statement was brief.

It confirmed very little and avoided almost everything else. A child had been found deceased. The investigation was ongoing. No additional information would be released at that time.

Those sentences were chosen carefully.

Behind them, the work had already begun.

The bag had been transported under supervision, sealed and logged. Every step was recorded. Times, names, conditions. The kind of documentation that looks clean on paper and heavy in practice. Officers spoke in lower voices now. The earlier neutrality had drained away, replaced by focus.

Inside the controlled environment of the examination room, the questions narrowed.

How old?

How long?

From where?

The answers did not arrive all at once.

Some things could be said quickly. The remains were those of a young child. The child had been deceased before being placed in the bag. The bag itself did not belong to the child. It had been used.

Other things took longer.

Investigators are trained to separate what they *know* from what they *suspect*. That line matters. Crossing it too early can collapse a case before it's built. So they stayed on the safe side of it, even as the weight of what lay before them pressed in.

There were no identifying items inside the bag. No clothing that pointed clearly to a school or neighborhood. No documents. No name written anywhere. Nothing that said, *This is who he was.*

The absence was immediate and unsettling.

Children usually leave traces. A record somewhere. A photograph. A teacher who remembers them. A doctor who has seen them. A neighbor who knows their name. Even children living on the margins tend to be tethered to something.

This child, for now, was not.

As preliminary assessments continued, investigators resisted the urge to speculate aloud. They worked with what could be established and set the rest aside. That restraint wasn't indifference. It was discipline.

Still, certain impressions formed quietly.

This was not a situation that suggested sudden chaos. There was nothing about the circumstances that pointed to an accident that spiraled. The condition of the remains did not align with a single moment gone wrong. Whatever had happened, it had not happened all at once.

That understanding stayed unspoken, but it shaped the room.

Outside, the story began to spread.

Reporters gathered at a distance. Cameras pointed toward the street where the bag had been found, now unremarkable again. People in the neighborhood talked in low tones. Some wondered aloud how they hadn't noticed anything earlier. Others insisted there was no way anyone could have known.

Both could be true.

Inside the investigation, the focus shifted to one urgent task: finding out who the child was.

Without a name, there could be no timeline. Without a timeline, there could be no accountability. The case could not move forward until the child moved out of anonymity.

Databases were checked. Missing child reports were cross-referenced. Recent cases were reviewed, then older ones. Nothing surfaced immediately. No obvious match. No immediate relief.

That silence was its own kind of answer.

It suggested the child had not been reported missing right away—or at all. It suggested delay. It suggested isolation. It suggested a life lived just outside the places where absence triggers alarms.

By the end of the day, investigators had confirmed what they could and withheld what they must.

They could say a child had died.

They could say an investigation was active.

They could say the public would be informed when appropriate.

What they could not yet say was who the child was, how long he had been gone, or why no one had stopped what led him here.

Those answers would come later.

For now, the case existed in a narrow space between discovery and understanding—a space filled with procedure, silence, and the growing realization that the hardest part of this story was not what had been found.

It was how long it might take to learn who had been missing.

CHAPTER 3 A CHILD WITHOUT A NAME

The first night passed without answers.

By morning, the case had a number, a lead investigator, and a growing file—but still no identity. That absence shaped everything that followed. Without a name, the child existed only as evidence. A body. A discovery. A problem to be solved.

Investigators began where they always do.

Missing persons databases were searched again, this time with broader parameters. Age ranges widened. Time frames stretched backward. Regional boundaries dissolved. They looked for reports that had gone quiet, cases that had stalled, names that had slipped past headlines.

Nothing matched cleanly.

That kind of silence is rare.

Children disappear loudly. Someone calls. Someone asks questions. Someone pushes until an answer arrives. Even in difficult circumstances, absence tends to leave ripples.

Here, there were none.

The next step was slower and more frustrating. Records that don't talk to each other. Systems that hold pieces but never the whole. School enrollments. Attendance lists. Medical encounters. Social service contacts. Each offered the possibility of recognition—and each came back empty or inconclusive.

The child had not appeared where children usually appear.

That did not mean he hadn't been seen.

It meant he had not been anchored.

Investigators began reaching outward. Quiet inquiries. Requests framed carefully to avoid contamination of memory. Had anyone noticed a child who stopped appearing? Had anyone seen a boy whose routines had changed without explanation?

People thought. People hesitated.

Some remembered something small. A child once seen at a window. A boy who stayed close to an adult's leg and didn't wander. A presence that didn't demand attention and therefore didn't receive much.

But memory without context is fragile.

No one could offer a name. No one could say when they last saw him with certainty. No one could explain where he went.

As the hours turned into days, the lack of a missing persons report became impossible to ignore. It meant no alarm had been raised. No official search had begun. No moment existed where the child's absence was treated as urgent.

That realization settled heavily.

It suggested that when the child vanished from daily view, his disappearance did not interrupt anyone's life enough to trigger action. It suggested that whatever world he had lived in was small —and that shrinking out of it did not register as an emergency.

Investigators had seen versions of this before.

Children living under control often leave fewer footprints. They move less. They interact with fewer people. Their worlds are managed tightly, which means fewer witnesses when something changes.

Anonymity, in those cases, is not an accident.

It is a condition.

As the search continued, the case began to attract attention beyond the immediate area. Media outlets repeated the same lines from official statements, careful not to speculate. Social media filled the gaps with guesses and theories, some well-meaning, others careless.

Still, no one came forward to claim the child.

No family member.

No caregiver.

No one asking questions on record.

The investigation now faced its first true obstacle.

Without a name, the child's life had to be reconstructed backward—through shadows, partial memories, and systems that had failed to capture him when it mattered. Every next step would depend on patience, restraint, and the willingness to sit with uncertainty.

The boy had existed.

That much was undeniable.

The question was how he had managed to exist so quietly that the world noticed him only after it was too late.

CHAPTER 4 SOMEONE HAD SEEN HIM

The first crack in the silence came from hesitation, not certainty.

It wasn't a dramatic tip or a confident identification. It was a call placed carefully, as if the person on the other end didn't want to overstep. They explained they weren't sure this mattered. That they might be mistaken. That they hadn't said anything earlier because nothing had seemed clearly wrong at the time.

Investigators listened anyway.

The caller described a child they had seen before—quiet, often close to an adult, rarely alone. The details were thin, but they lingered in ways that mattered. A height estimate. A vague age range. A memory of stillness.

It wasn't enough to identify the child.

But it was enough to confirm he had been seen.

That changed the shape of the case.

As word spread through controlled channels, more fragments

surfaced. Not all at once. Slowly. Unevenly. Each piece arrived wrapped in uncertainty, offered with disclaimers.

I don't know if this helps.

I might be remembering wrong.

It didn't feel serious then.

A neighbor recalled seeing a boy occasionally but couldn't place exactly when. He was never outside alone. Never loud. Never disruptive. The kind of child who blends into the background, especially in places where people mind their own business.

Another person remembered a moment that stood out only because it hadn't stood out at the time. A child lingering behind an adult, eyes lowered, answering questions quietly or not at all. Nothing alarming enough to justify interference. Just a feeling—easy to dismiss.

Investigators recognized the pattern immediately.

These were not witnesses to an event. They were witnesses to a presence.

The challenge with presence is that it leaves no timestamp. It doesn't demand documentation. It relies on memory, and memory softens quickly when nothing forces it to harden.

As inquiries continued, attention turned to institutions that might have intersected with the child's life. Schools. Clinics. Services. Places where adults are trained to notice children.

A teacher came forward, uncertain. There had been a student, maybe. Attendance had been inconsistent. The child had been withdrawn but not disruptive. There were moments that felt off, but nothing concrete enough to escalate.

Nothing that crossed the line.

That phrase surfaced repeatedly.

It didn't cross the line.

Investigators understood what that meant. Lines are drawn

to protect against false accusations, but they can also become barriers. When harm lives just beneath them, it goes unchallenged.

Each person who had seen the child carried a version of the same explanation: they hadn't known enough. They hadn't wanted to be wrong. They hadn't felt justified in acting.

None of them believed they were ignoring danger.

They believed they were being careful.

As these accounts accumulated, a painful clarity emerged. The child had not been invisible. He had been visible in fragments— seen briefly, known vaguely, remembered imperfectly.

No one had seen enough to feel responsible.

And because responsibility never settled anywhere, it dissolved everywhere.

By the end of the week, investigators were no longer asking whether the child had been seen.

They were asking how many people had noticed something small and chosen silence because it felt safer than speaking without certainty.

The silence around the child had not been absolute.

It had been shared.

CHAPTER 5 A HOME THAT LOOKED NORMAL

From the outside, there was nothing to stop the eye.

The house blended into the street the way most houses do —intentionally unremarkable. No broken windows. No visible damage. No signs that suggested urgency or disorder. It was the kind of place people passed every day without a second glance.

That ordinariness mattered more than anyone realized at the time.

When investigators began tracing the child's last known environment, they were met first with appearances. A lived-in home. Basic utilities functioning. Furniture in place. Nothing that demanded immediate alarm. Nothing that forced confrontation.

In systems designed to respond to crisis, this is where danger often hides.

Inside, the space carried the quiet of routine. Objects arranged with purpose. Surfaces kept clean enough to suggest control. There was no chaos to point toward neglect, no obvious evidence of collapse. Everything communicated a version of stability.

Investigators are trained to notice what doesn't fit—but they are also human. First impressions shape tone. They influence how questions are framed, how answers are received, and how deeply skepticism is applied.

And this place offered reassurance.

Caregivers who harm children rarely do so in environments that advertise it. Disorder draws attention. Attention invites questions. Questions threaten control. So control is maintained through appearance—through the performance of normal life.

In this home, explanations came easily.

Schedules were described calmly. Behaviors were contextualized. Any irregularities were softened with reasonable explanations that sounded familiar. A missed appointment became a misunderstanding. A withdrawn child became shy. A change in routine became temporary.

None of these explanations were implausible.

That was the problem.

Clean spaces carry authority. They tell systems that someone is capable. That things are being handled. When a home looks functional, concern has to work harder to justify itself. Doubt feels impolite. Skepticism feels accusatory.

So outsiders accept what they see.

Neighbors hadn't questioned the household. Interactions were brief, polite, uneventful. Nothing loud enough to provoke action. Nothing dramatic enough to lodge in memory. The child did not roam. He did not draw attention. He stayed close, quiet, managed.

To an outside observer, that can look like care.

To investigators, looking back, it looked like control.

This is how harm survives without chaos. Not by hiding everything, but by hiding just enough. By keeping life predictable. By ensuring no single moment demands escalation.

The danger of a "normal" home is that it trains people to trust their eyes more than their instincts. It tells them that whatever they don't understand probably has a reasonable explanation. It reassures them that intervention would be unnecessary—maybe even unfair.

By the time investigators began to question what had been happening inside those walls, the illusion had already done its work.

The home had looked normal long enough for silence to settle in.

And inside that silence, the child remained unprotected.

CHAPTER 7 THE LAST TIME HE WAS SEEN

No one marked the moment when it happened.

There was no pause, no sense that something important had just passed. The last confirmed sighting of the child slipped into memory the way ordinary moments do—unremarkable at the time, almost invisible in retrospect.

That is often how endings arrive.

The sighting itself was brief. A child near an adult. A routine movement through a familiar space. Nothing loud. Nothing that would have made anyone stop and stare. The kind of moment that blends into the rhythm of daily life and leaves no immediate trace behind it.

Later, investigators would work carefully to anchor it. A place. An approximate time. A person who could say, with some confidence, *Yes, I saw him then.* But certainty was thin, and it had to be handled gently. Memory hardens only when it's challenged, and by the time questions were asked, the moment had already softened.

What stood out most was how ordinary it had been.

There was no visible distress. No struggle. No scene that demanded intervention. The child did not cry out. He did not run. He did not draw attention to himself. He existed quietly in that moment, the way he seemed to exist in many moments—present, but contained.

Afterward, nothing changed fast enough to raise alarm.

Days passed without a report. No search began. No one came asking questions. Life continued around the absence as if absence itself had not yet arrived. For those who had seen the child, there was no reason to connect that brief encounter to anything larger.

At the time, it was just a memory among many.

Only later did it acquire weight.

When investigators returned to the people who might have crossed paths with the child, they encountered a familiar discomfort. Faces tightened. Voices slowed. People tried to recall details that hadn't mattered before. They replayed moments, searching for meaning they hadn't recognized when it was still possible to act.

This is where guilt settles in—not because someone ignored something obvious, but because the obvious only reveals itself in hindsight.

Someone wondered if the child had looked tired. Another remembered how quiet he had been. Another questioned whether the adult beside him had seemed tense. None of these details had been clear warnings. All of them felt heavier once the ending was known.

Silence followed the last sighting, but not the kind that feels intentional.

It was the silence of routine. Of days blending together. Of no single disruption forcing awareness. The child did not vanish publicly. He faded privately, step by step, until no one could point to the moment when disappearance became real.

Investigators understood that silence well.

It is not always proof of concealment. Sometimes it is simply the result of a life lived close to the margins—where movement is limited, contact is controlled, and visibility is optional.

But silence has consequences either way.

Once the child passed beyond the point of being seen, everything that followed had to be reconstructed without him. No testimony. No explanation. No chance to interrupt what came next.

The last sighting did not feel like an ending.

That is what made it one.

CHAPTER 8 REPORTS THAT WENT NOWHERE

By the time the investigation reached this stage, it was no longer focused only on what had happened.

It was focused on what *hadn't*.

Investigators began pulling records that weren't supposed to matter much on their own. Call logs. Notes. Entries that existed without fanfare. The kind of documentation that accumulates quietly in systems built to handle volume rather than nuance.

What emerged was not a trail that led cleanly forward.

It was a circle.

There had been contact. Not once, not loudly, but enough to register. Calls placed without urgency. Concerns voiced cautiously, framed with uncertainty. Nothing that demanded immediate action. Nothing that carried the language of crisis.

The reports had landed where many reports do.

They were acknowledged.

They were logged.

And then they stalled.

Follow-up is where intervention either begins or dies. In this case, it softened into delay. Time passed without escalation. No second visit. No urgent check. No moment where concern hardened into action.

On paper, the system appeared responsive. There were timestamps. Names. Notes indicating awareness. But awareness alone does not interrupt harm. It only documents that someone noticed something and did not know what to do with it.

As investigators traced these reports backward, they noticed the language used to describe them.

Careful. Neutral. Noncommittal.

Words that protected against error also protected against urgency. Each entry allowed room for doubt, and doubt created space for inaction.

Behind the paperwork were people stretched thin.

Caseworkers managing more families than they could reasonably track. Priorities set by visible danger. Decisions made quickly, often with incomplete information. In those conditions, subtle cases fall behind louder ones.

Not because they are unimportant.

Because they are quiet.

Quiet cases do not compete well.

Some files showed signs of movement that went nowhere. A concern flagged, then resolved on paper without resolution in reality. A follow-up attempted, then delayed. A decision to wait for more information that never arrived.

Eventually, the case drifted.

Not formally closed, but no longer active enough to protect anyone.

This is how cases disappear inside systems without anyone choosing to abandon them. There is no dramatic ending. Just a gradual loss of momentum until attention moves elsewhere.

Responsibility thinned as it spread.

A caller assumed someone else would take over. A professional assumed another agency had deeper involvement. Systems overlapped without aligning, each holding a fragment and trusting that the whole existed somewhere else.

It didn't.

When investigators laid the pieces side by side, the shape became clearer. Reports had existed. Concern had surfaced. The system had responded—but not decisively enough to change the child's circumstances.

No one had ignored him outright.

They had processed him.

And in doing so, they allowed time to continue moving forward without interruption, carrying the child toward an ending that no report, on its own, was strong enough to stop.

CHAPTER 9 RED FLAGS

By the time investigators began to look across everything at once, the case started to feel less like a mystery and more like a pattern that had been hiding in plain sight.

Not a single warning missed—but many warnings softened.

Early concerns that had once seemed isolated began to echo each other. A note here. A comment there. An observation made and then set aside. None of them dramatic. None of them definitive. All of them pointing in roughly the same direction without ever converging.

Individually, they were easy to dismiss.

Together, they were harder to ignore.

Some concerns had been raised and then quietly resolved with explanations that felt reasonable at the time. A bruise that had a story. A behavioral change that could be attributed to stress or instability. A missed appointment that didn't repeat often enough to demand escalation.

People had wanted to believe the explanations.

Belief is powerful. It keeps systems moving. It prevents unnecessary disruption. It reassures professionals that restraint is the same as fairness. But belief, when unchallenged, can also become paralysis.

Risk assessments reflected that hesitation.

They weighed what was visible, what was reported, and what could be proven. When evidence was incomplete, the assessment leaned conservative. When caregivers appeared cooperative, risk diminished on paper. When environments looked functional, danger seemed less immediate.

The child remained in the margins of concern.

What stood in the way again and again was the absence of proof.

"No proof" sounded responsible. It protected against overreach. It guarded against false accusation. It justified waiting.

But waiting required the situation to stay still.

It didn't.

As investigators revisited the records, they could see how the demand for certainty had worked against the child. Harm that unfolds gradually rarely produces proof all at once. It reveals itself in fragments, and fragments are easy to dismiss when systems are designed to respond to clarity, not accumulation.

There was also fear.

Fear of stepping beyond authority. Fear of acting without confirmation. Fear of being wrong and facing consequences for it. These fears weren't abstract—they were shaped by real professional risk. People had learned where the boundaries were, and they stayed inside them.

Caution was rewarded.

Intervention was risky.

So concern lingered instead of advancing.

The cost of that waiting became clear only in retrospect. Time had passed. Details had faded. Records had grown stale. Opportunities for early interruption had slipped away quietly, without a moment that clearly marked their passing.

What investigators came to understand was not that the red flags had been invisible.

They had been visible—but never visible enough, never persistent enough, never gathered tightly enough to force action.

Consequences never followed.

And without consequences, the warnings lost their power, leaving the child exactly where he had been—unprotected, unseen in ways that mattered, and moving steadily toward an ending no single red flag was ever strong enough to prevent.

CHAPTER 10 THE VISIT THAT CHANGED NOTHING

It was meant to be a safeguard.

A scheduled visit. An official presence. The kind of step that exists to interrupt harm before it deepens. On paper, it looked like progress—evidence that concern had been acknowledged and addressed.

In reality, it became something else.

The visit was brief. Structured. Contained by time and expectation. The person who arrived had a checklist, a mandate to observe, and limited authority to act beyond what could be immediately justified.

From the beginning, the tone was controlled.

There were no raised voices. No visible tension. The environment appeared stable enough to discourage alarm. Questions were answered calmly. Explanations were offered before they were fully formed. Nothing about the interaction demanded confrontation.

Observation, in that context, became passive.

The home did not present itself as a crisis. There were no obvious hazards. No signs of collapse. The child remained close, quiet, managed. His presence did not interrupt the narrative being offered on his behalf.

That mattered more than anyone realized.

In situations like this, what is seen often outweighs what is felt. Instinct hesitates when it cannot justify itself with facts. And facts, during short visits, are limited to surfaces.

The questions that mattered most were not asked.

Not because they were unknown, but because asking them would have required pushing past politeness, past cooperation, past the appearance of normalcy. They would have required slowing the moment down and risking conflict without certainty.

Instead, the visit stayed within safe boundaries.

Notes were taken. Observations recorded. Language remained careful. Nothing rose to the level that demanded immediate action. The visit concluded without escalation, without a clear reason to return urgently.

On paper, the system had done its job.

In practice, nothing had changed.

Afterward, the file did not close—but it did not move forward either. The moment that could have altered the trajectory passed quietly, absorbed into routine.

Looking back, it is tempting to name this visit as the turning point —the place where intervention failed.

But that framing is too simple.

This visit was not the only opportunity. It was one of several. And like the others, it was shaped by uncertainty, by limited authority, by the belief that restraint was responsibility.

The most damaging assumption was not that nothing was wrong.

It was that nothing was wrong *enough*.

That assumption allowed the visit to end without consequence. It allowed the child to remain where he was. It allowed time to continue moving forward without interruption.

When investigators later returned to this moment, they did not find negligence in the traditional sense. They found hesitation. They found caution. They found a system doing exactly what it was designed to do—responding to what could be proven, not what was suspected.

The visit did not change anything.

And because it didn't, it quietly became one more step on a path that was already narrowing toward an outcome no one present could yet see—or was prepared to name.

CHAPTER 11 HOW ABUSE HID

Nothing about the child's life suggested chaos from a distance.

There were no repeated emergencies. No public breakdowns. No moments that demanded attention from outside the home. What existed instead was control—steady, quiet, and effective.

Control does not need noise to work.

It begins with predictability. Rules that shift without warning. Consequences that are never fully explained. A child learns quickly how to avoid disruption by minimizing themselves. They learn when to speak and when silence is safer. Over time, this learning becomes instinct.

Fear, in this context, is not always dramatic. It doesn't announce itself. It settles into routine. It teaches a child to scan tone and posture, to anticipate reactions before they happen. The goal is not punishment—it is compliance.

From the outside, this can look like good behavior.

Inside, it feels like vigilance.

Isolation deepens that control.

The child's world was small. Contact with others was limited and managed. Time outside the home did not follow consistent patterns. Opportunities for unsupervised interaction were rare. When adults did encounter the child, those moments were brief and incomplete.

Isolation does not require locked doors.

It only requires enough separation that no one sees the whole picture. A teacher sees a behavior. A neighbor sees a presence. A professional sees an environment. Each fragment looks manageable on its own.

Together, they would have told a different story.

Children in these situations rarely disclose openly. Not because they don't want help, but because disclosure is dangerous when survival depends on control. A child tests safety before telling the truth. They offer pieces. They watch reactions. If nothing changes —or if consequences follow—they learn to stop trying.

Silence becomes strategy.

Adults often misunderstand this silence. They interpret it as resilience, shyness, or emotional distance. They assume that a child who doesn't complain must be coping.

But silence is not absence of suffering.

It is evidence of adaptation.

Control extends outward as well.

Caregivers who harm children often shape how other adults perceive them. They speak confidently. They provide explanations quickly. They appear cooperative and composed. They frame the child in ways that soften concern—difficult, sensitive, clumsy, dramatic.

None of these labels sound alarming on their own.

They shift attention away from harm and toward interpretation.

As doubt spreads, urgency fades. People hesitate. They wait. They choose not to push without proof. The caregiver's narrative fills the space where questions might have grown.

This is how abuse hides without secrecy.

Not behind locked doors, but behind credibility.

Not through constant fear, but through controlled normalcy.

The child learns to disappear in plain sight—not physically, but emotionally. Needs are suppressed. Signals grow subtle. Distress becomes quiet enough to pass unnoticed.

By the time investigators began to understand how completely the child's world had been managed, the damage had already been done.

Abuse did not hide because no one was looking.

It hid because looking never lasted long enough—and because silence, once learned, did exactly what it was meant to do.

It kept the child alive just long enough to remain unseen.

CHAPTER 12 THE FINAL DAYS

The final days did not announce themselves.

There was no clear marker separating them from the days that came before. No visible shift that would have signaled an ending was approaching. Life, such as it was, continued within its narrow boundaries—controlled, quiet, contained.

Investigators would later work carefully to determine what could be known about this period and what could not. They approached it with restraint, aware that certainty was limited and that speculation could do more harm than good.

What could be established came from evidence, not assumption.

Timelines narrowed. Movements were approximated. Interactions were inferred cautiously. Nothing suggested a sudden crisis erupting out of nowhere. Instead, the final days appeared to fit into a pattern that had already been unfolding—one marked by isolation and control.

Some details were clear enough to matter.

The child had not been seen outside the home during this time. There were no confirmed sightings that contradicted that understanding. Contact with others had ceased, or at least narrowed to the point of invisibility. Whatever routines had once existed had quietly ended.

This absence raised questions that could not be answered directly.

Investigators resisted the urge to fill those gaps with narrative. They knew better than to impose a story where facts were thin. Instead, they allowed the silence itself to remain part of the record.

The body provided information, though only in fragments.

It did not explain motive or sequence. It did not tell a complete story. It did, however, suggest continuity—conditions that develop over time rather than in a single moment. That distinction mattered. It confirmed that what happened at the end could not be separated from what had come before.

The final days were not an isolated event.

They were the last stretch of a longer reality.

Certain details were withheld deliberately. Not everything investigators learned was released publicly, and not everything they chose to withhold was dramatic. Some information offered no clarity beyond what was already known. Other details, while painful, did not advance understanding.

Restraint was not avoidance.

It was respect.

In cases involving children, there is a line between informing and exposing. Investigators stayed on the side of that line that preserved dignity, even as public curiosity intensified.

As the picture of the final days settled, it became clear that intervention was no longer possible by the time this period began. The chance to stop what was happening had existed earlier—spread across missed warnings, deferred decisions, and moments when silence had prevailed.

By the time the final days arrived, the trajectory was already set.

There was no dramatic collapse. No sudden turn that could have been interrupted with one timely action. The ending unfolded quietly, within the same constraints that had defined the child's life.

What investigators were left with was not a single moment to point to, but an understanding that the final days were the result of everything that had been allowed to continue unchecked.

And that understanding carried a weight no report could fully capture.

Because the most difficult truth was not how the story ended.

It was how long it had been allowed to go on.

CHAPTER 13 THE MOMENT IT ENDED

There were no witnesses to the moment itself.

No one saw the exact point where the child's life stopped. No sound carried far enough to be heard. No interruption came from outside the walls that had contained him for so long. Whatever happened occurred in isolation, without the presence of anyone who could intervene.

That absence would define everything that followed.

Investigators would later search for markers—times, movements, actions that could be fixed with certainty. But the moment resisted precision. It existed somewhere within a narrow window, shaped by what could be ruled out rather than what could be confirmed.

The ending was quiet.

Not dramatic. Not chaotic. It did not resemble the scenes people imagine when they think of violence. It arrived the way prolonged neglect often does—without spectacle, without resistance, without anyone stepping in to change its course.

There was no intervention because there was no one there to intervene.

The systems that might have interrupted this moment had already receded. The visits were over. The reports had gone still. The concerns had softened into records. By the time the end arrived, the child was beyond the reach of every safeguard that had once hovered at the edges of his life.

There was no second chance.

Children do not get retries. There is no recovery window after the fact, no opportunity to undo what has already happened. When neglect reaches its final point, it does so without warning, leaving behind a permanence that cannot be negotiated.

What makes this moment especially difficult to confront is how ordinary it was allowed to be.

There was no final argument overheard. No dramatic escalation captured on record. The conditions that led to the ending had been in place for so long that the end itself did not disrupt the environment around it.

Neglect had done what neglect often does.

It closed in slowly, then completely.

Only later, with distance and hindsight, did the weight of that finality become clear. Every earlier hesitation suddenly carried consequence. Every deferred decision took on gravity. Every moment where action had felt premature now looked painfully overdue.

Investigators could document the outcome.

They could establish cause.

They could place the moment within a timeline.

But they could not give the child back the protection he had been denied.

LINDA DAVIDSON

The moment it ended did not announce itself to the world.

It waited until discovery forced recognition.

And by then, the silence that had surrounded the child for so long had already done its work—leaving behind an ending that could be named, recorded, and investigated, but never undone.

CHAPTER 14 THE INVESTIGATION SHIFTS

The discovery forced the case into motion.

What had once moved cautiously now moved under pressure. The focus narrowed. The pace quickened. An investigation that had been shaped by uncertainty was suddenly defined by urgency.

The child was no longer an abstraction.

He was evidence.

Additional personnel were brought in. Agencies that had once worked in parallel began sharing information directly. Records were reexamined. Old notes were reread with new attention. What had once seemed minor now carried weight it hadn't been given before.

Timelines began to collide.

Statements that had sounded consistent early on no longer

aligned perfectly. Small discrepancies surfaced—dates that didn't quite match, details that shifted depending on who was speaking and when. These inconsistencies were not dramatic, but they mattered. They suggested memory under strain, narratives adjusting to scrutiny, or something being withheld.

Investigators did not rush to conclusions.

They allowed the pressure to do its work.

As the case tightened, stories changed subtly. Explanations grew more detailed. Certain facts were emphasized while others were quietly minimized. People who had once spoken freely became guarded. Others became more talkative than necessary.

Investigators are trained to notice both.

The evidence that existed before the discovery was now examined differently. Items once treated as routine were reconsidered. Notes that had felt sufficient at the time were reevaluated for what they lacked rather than what they contained.

The frustration was not about missing information.

It was about timing.

So much of what now mattered had been available earlier—just not treated as urgent. The shift in perspective did not create new evidence. It changed how existing evidence was understood.

Public attention intensified.

The neighborhood watched. The media waited. Questions pressed against official silence. Authorities balanced transparency with restraint, aware that premature disclosure could compromise the case.

Inside the investigation, the focus narrowed further.

This was no longer a question of *what happened* in general terms.

It was a question of responsibility.

Who knew what, and when?

Who acted, and who didn't?

Where did concern stall, and why?

The investigation had crossed a line.

It was no longer only about discovery.

It was about accountability—both personal and institutional—and the uncomfortable reality that once a case reaches this stage, some truths surface too late to change the outcome they reveal.

The work continued.

But it did so under the shadow of a fact that could not be undone: the urgency that now defined the investigation had arrived only after the child was already gone.

CHAPTER 15
ACCOUNTABILITY

Accountability arrived slowly.

Not as a single decision or a clear declaration, but as a series of careful steps taken under scrutiny. Once the investigation shifted toward responsibility, every move carried weight. Every word was chosen deliberately. Every action was measured against what could be proven—not what felt obvious in hindsight.

Charges were considered with restraint.

Investigators and prosecutors examined what the evidence could support, not what the public expected. The distinction mattered. Suspicion alone was not enough. Timelines had to hold. Actions had to be specific. Intent had to be established within the limits of the law.

This process was methodical and unsatisfying to watch.

The law does not move at the pace of outrage. It moves at the pace of proof.

As decisions were made, legal limitations surfaced. Some failures did not fit neatly into criminal statutes. Some actions—or inactions—fell into spaces where responsibility was diffuse rather than concentrated. Neglect, when prolonged and layered, can be devastating without producing a single moment that qualifies as a prosecutable act.

This gap between moral responsibility and legal accountability became impossible to ignore.

Institutions responded in parallel.

Statements were released acknowledging tragedy without assigning fault. Internal reviews were announced. Language emphasized policy, procedure, and cooperation. The tone was solemn, but careful. No one rushed to claim error. No one admitted failure outright.

The words mattered.

They were crafted to inform without exposing, to reassure without conceding. Each sentence balanced empathy with distance. Each phrase reflected an awareness that this case carried consequences beyond one child—it touched systems, roles, and reputations.

Public frustration grew.

People wanted names. They wanted certainty. They wanted to know who would answer for what had happened. But accountability narrowed as it moved forward, attaching itself only to what could be firmly established.

Responsibility, once spread across many hands, became difficult to pin down.

This was not because no one bore responsibility.

It was because responsibility had been diluted over time—shared among decisions that seemed reasonable in isolation and devastating in accumulation.

By the time formal accountability took shape, it felt incomplete.

Not wrong.

Incomplete.

The process answered some questions while leaving others unresolved. It clarified legal outcomes without fully addressing how a child could pass through so many points of contact without being protected.

What remained was a quiet reckoning.

Justice, in this case, did not arrive as closure. It arrived as structure—rules followed, steps taken, outcomes recorded. It did what the law allows it to do.

But the space between what was allowed and what was needed remained.

And in that space, the question lingered—not as an accusation, but as an unresolved truth:

Who answers when accountability is shared so widely that it belongs to everyone, and therefore to no one at all?

CHAPTER 16 THE CHILD NO ONE STOPPED

The case reached its end without delivering comfort.

Files were closed. Timelines finalized. Statements archived. What remained was not resolution, but weight—the kind that settles after everything that can be done has already been done.

At the center of it all was the child himself.

Not the evidence.

Not the headlines.

Not the case number.

A child who had lived quietly, moved carefully, and existed within limits he did not choose.

In the records, his life appeared in fragments. Dates without stories. Notes without context. Mentions without continuity. The investigation had pieced together what it could, but even at its most complete, the picture felt unfinished.

Because the most important parts of his life were the ones never recorded.

He had been more than a problem to solve. More than a responsibility deferred. He had been someone who woke up, who waited, who learned what was safe to expect and what was not. Someone who adapted to his surroundings the way children do— by becoming smaller when the world feels dangerous.

That is what makes the failure so difficult to confront.

Nothing about his suffering required extraordinary cruelty to persist. It survived on ordinary decisions. On politeness. On hesitation. On the belief that someone else would step in if things were truly wrong.

At every level, there had been an opportunity to interrupt what was happening.

Not one dramatic moment, but many small ones. Moments when a question could have been asked differently. When uncertainty could have leaned toward caution instead of restraint. When discomfort could have been accepted as necessary rather than avoided.

None of those moments felt decisive at the time.

That is how harm endures.

The patterns revealed in this case were not unique. Investigators recognized them because they had seen them before—children living just beyond the edges of visibility, systems responding without connecting, concern circulating without settling anywhere long enough to force action.

This case did not introduce those patterns.

It exposed them.

What ultimately failed the child was not the absence of care in the abstract, but the absence of interruption. No one stopped the slow narrowing of his world. No one broke the silence that had become his environment.

By the time the truth was undeniable, the chance to protect him no longer existed.

Remembering him requires more than acknowledging what happened.

It requires sitting with the reality that his life ended not because help was impossible, but because it never arrived soon enough to matter. That his suffering did not go unseen, but unchallenged. That silence, once shared widely enough, can feel like normalcy.

The child did not disappear all at once.

He was missed gradually.

And when the world finally stopped for him, it was only to document what had already been lost.

That is the ending this case leaves behind.

Not closure.

Not reassurance.

Just the quiet, irreversible truth of a child who should have been stopped—and wasn't.

EPILOGUE

After everything ends, the places remain.

The street where the bag was found returns to its rhythm. Footsteps pass. Cars move through. The ordinary sounds of a city reclaim the space as if nothing extraordinary ever happened there. To anyone who wasn't paying attention that day, there is no marker to suggest what it briefly held.

Investigations leave behind paperwork, not monuments.

The case file becomes part of an archive—referenced occasionally, cited carefully, then folded back into the larger system that continues forward. New cases arrive. New urgencies demand attention. The machinery does not stop, even when the reason it moved in the first place is gone.

But stories like this don't end when the system finishes with them.

They linger in quieter ways.

They surface when someone hesitates before dismissing a concern. When a teacher pauses longer over a pattern that doesn't quite fit. When a neighbor decides that uncertainty is not a reason to stay silent. When a professional feels the pull of restraint and chooses, instead, to press once more.

The child at the center of this story will never know those moments.

He will never know whether his life changed how others see. Whether his absence sharpened attention somewhere else. Whether his ending interrupted another quiet trajectory before it reached the same place.

What he leaves behind is not instruction.

It is recognition.

Recognition that harm does not always hide behind extremes. That it can exist inside normal routines and clean spaces. That it survives not because people don't care, but because care is often deferred until it feels safe, certain, and justified.

In this case, certainty arrived too late.

The weight of that truth is not meant to be resolved. It is meant to be carried. Not as guilt for those who never knew him, but as awareness that protection rarely begins with proof—it begins with interruption.

Someone choosing to act before the story becomes complete.

The child no one stopped does not need to be remembered as a symbol.

He was not an idea or a lesson. He was a child whose life narrowed quietly while the world looked away just enough to miss it. Honoring him means resisting the comfort of believing this was rare, unrepeatable, or fully explained.

It means accepting that the most dangerous silence is the one shared by many people who each believe they don't know enough to speak.

The story ends here.

But the responsibility it exposes does not.

It continues wherever a child exists at the edge of notice—seen briefly, known vaguely, and waiting, without knowing it, for someone to decide that uncertainty is not a reason to do nothing.

ALSO IN THE SERIES

The Children the World Missed

Before this child was erased, there was another—found without a name, without answers, and without anyone left to speak for him.

The Boy in the Box: America's Unknown Child and the Case That Wouldn't Die examines one of the most haunting cases in American history: a young boy discovered abandoned, unidentified, and unclaimed—despite nationwide attention.There were witnesses who hesitated.Leads that stalled.
A city that searched, but too late.This investigation follows the decades-long effort to restore identity to a child the world noticed only after he was gone, and asks why recognition so often arrives after protection is no longer possible.

Read ***The Boy in the Box*** to begin ***The Children the World Missed***—a true crime series focused not on killers, but on the silence, delay, and human decisions that allowed children to vanish in plain sight.

Tap here to read The Boy in the Box: America's Unknown Child and the Case That Wouldn't Die

—or scan the QR code below to continue.

A PERSONAL REQUEST

Thank you for reading **The Child No One Stopped: The True Crime Story of Damari Carter**.

If this book stayed with you, I would be truly grateful if you left a review. Even a simple star rating—without writing anything—helps more than you might realize. It signals to Amazon and other platforms that this story matters, and that Damari's name deserves to be remembered.

If you'd like to leave a review, you can visit the Amazon page here:*The Child No One Stopped: The True Crime Story of Damari Carter*

Or simply scan the QR code below to go directly to the review page.

Your support helps ensure **Damari Carter's** story—and the stories of children too often overlooked—are not forgotten.

With gratitude,

Linda Davidson

NEXT IN THE SERIES…

If you're reading this as part of the trilogy of cases:
- **The Boy in the Box**
- **The Boy in a Suitcase**
- **The Child No One Stopped**

(Reading order is flexible, but themes deepen when read as a set.)

ALSO BY LINDA DAVIDSON

1. Don't Let Me Die Here: The Lars Mittank Case — A True Story of Disappearance, Fear, and a Mother's Unbreakable Hope
2. The Vanished Heiress: Agatha Christie's Eleven Days of Silence
3. Without a Trace: The Cold silence of Maura Murray
4. Charming the Darkness: The Rodney Alcala Case
5. Whispers Along the Parkway: The Unsolved Murders That Haunt America's Cradle of History
6. *Vanished on the Open Road: The Gabby Petito Story*
7. Bloodline Broken: The Fall of the Murdaugh Dynasty
8. Buried in the Sand: Thirteen Victims. One Quiet Monster. A Decade of Silence
9. *Stolen Faces: The Man Who Became the Missing*
10. *The Glamour Grift: How Anna Delvey Fooled the Rich and Faked Her Empire*
11. *The Last Mile He Walked: A True Story of Loss, Confusion and The Disappearance of Brandon Swanson*
12. *Tracks to Nowhere: The Mysterious Death of Tiffany Valiante*
13. *Buried in Belief : The Shocking Crimes of Lori Vallow and Chad Daybell*
14. *Tracks to Nowhere: The Mysterious Death of Tiffany Valiante*
15. *Silent Blocks: The Disappearance of Jason Jolkowski and the Walk He Never Finished*

16. *Vanished in the Pines: The Disappearance of DeOrr Kunz Jr. and the Secrets Beneath Timber Creek*
17. *The Girl in Room 2805: The Grisly Mystery of Elisa Lam*
18. *Rolled in Silence : The Kendrick Johnson Story*
19. *Eyes of the Devil: The Crimes of Richard Ramirez, The Night Stalker*
20. *The Man Who Wasn't There : D.B. Cooper and The Skyjacker's Disappearance Act*
21. *Daughters of the Cult: Warren Jeffs and the Children of Silence*

ABOUT THE AUTHOR

Linda Davidson is a true crime author who writes for readers who want more than shock value — they want truth with a heartbeat.

She focuses on the kinds of stories that stay with you long after the news cameras leave: unsolved murders, missing persons, rural disappearances, and investigations that never received clear answers. Instead of chasing sensational headlines, Linda writes with one question in mind: *How can I honor the victim and still tell the full truth of what happened?*

In each book, she blends careful research, clear timelines, and compassionate storytelling. Readers are guided through evidence, leads, theories, and dead ends in a way that is easy to follow and emotionally grounded. Her work keeps the victim at the center of the narrative while also examining the failures, gaps, and human decisions that shaped each case.

Linda's books are written for true crime readers who care about people, not just plot twists. She writes for those who feel frustrated by shallow coverage and are hungry for deeper, more thoughtful explorations of the cases that haunt them.

Her promise is simple:

She will research carefully.

She will explain clearly.

She will tell the truth with respect.

She will never forget that the people she writes about were real.

Linda Davidson is a true crime author dedicated to telling the stories others forget. She writes about unsolved murders, mysterious disappearances, and cold cases with a focus on the victims, their families, and the communities left behind. Combining deep research with compassionate storytelling, she helps readers make sense of complex investigations without losing sight of the human beings at the center of every case.

IF YOU ARE WORRIED ABOUT A CHILD

If you believe a child is in danger, contact emergency services in your country.

United States

- Emergency: **911**
- Childhelp National Child Abuse Hotline (24/7): **1-800-4-A-CHILD (1-800-422-4453)**

If you are outside the U.S., search for your local child protection reporting line or emergency number. You do not need absolute proof to raise a concern.

CONTENT NOTE

This book involves the death of a child and themes of abuse, neglect, and system failure. Graphic descriptions are avoided, but the subject matter may be distressing. Please take breaks as needed and prioritize your wellbeing.

Respect and Restraint

In writing this book, I avoided:

- sensationalized detail
- speculation presented as fact
- unnecessary descriptions that do not advance understanding

The child at the center of this story is treated as a human life, not a plot device.

AUTHOR'S MESSAGE TO THE READER

Thank you for reading with care.

If this story stayed with you, that is not weakness—it is evidence of empathy. True crime should never numb us. It should sharpen attention, deepen discernment, and remind us that the most vulnerable often depend on ordinary people choosing to act early.

— **Linda Davidson**

ACKNOWLEDGEMENT

True crime is possible because of people who document the truth: investigators, forensic professionals, journalists, advocates, and community members who choose to speak despite discomfort or fear.

I also acknowledge readers who approach true crime with care. Witnessing difficult stories—especially those involving children—requires emotional courage.

Most of all, I acknowledge the child at the center of this book. He mattered long before this story existed.

AUTHOR'S NOTE

Thank you for reading *The Child No One Stopped*.

This book was written with a deliberate restraint. When the victim is a child, there is a thin line between bearing witness and turning suffering into spectacle. I chose to stay on the side of dignity—focusing on what can be responsibly described, and refusing to fill gaps with dramatic certainty where the public record is incomplete.

True crime often promises closure. Real life rarely delivers it. What it can deliver—when handled carefully—is clarity, accountability where possible, and remembrance that refuses to reduce a child to a case number.

If this book left you unsettled, that response is human. Some stories are heavy not because of graphic detail, but because of what they reveal about silence, delay, and the way harm can hide inside ordinary life.

— **Linda Davidson**

DISCLAIMER

This book is a work of narrative nonfiction based on publicly available information.

Every effort has been made to present events accurately and responsibly. However:

- Some details may remain uncertain due to sealed records, incomplete reporting, or conflicting accounts.
- The author makes no claim to have access to non-public investigative files.
- All individuals are presumed innocent unless proven guilty in a court of law.
- This book is not legal, medical, or professional advice.

Any errors are unintentional. Credible corrections may be addressed in future editions.

SOURCES AND RESEARCH NOTES

This book draws on publicly available sources, which may include:
- law enforcement statements and press briefings
- reputable news reporting
- court updates where accessible
- official agency publications and background resources

Because reporting and legal proceedings can evolve, later updates may clarify or revise early information.

REFERENCES

Associated Press. (2024, March 6). Remains of child found in duffel bag in Philadelphia neighborhood identified as missing boy. *AP News.*

https://apnews.com/article/philadelphia-duffel-bag-child-remains-identified-damari-carter

Associated Press. (2024, March 7). Mother, boyfriend charged in death of 4-year-old boy whose body was found in duffel bag. *AP News.*

https://apnews.com/article/damari-carter-philadelphia-child-duffel-bag-charges

Phillipp, C. (2024, March 6). Body found in duffel bag ID'd as missing 4-year-old boy; mother and boyfriend charged. *People.*

https://people.com/body-found-duffel-bag-idd-missing-4-year-old-boy-mother-boyfriend-charged-8606405

CBS News. (2024, March 7). Mom, boyfriend charged after body of missing 4-year-old found in duffel bag in Philadelphia. *CBS News.*

https://www.cbsnews.com/news/damari-carter-philadelphia-duffel-bag-mother-boyfriend-charged/

NBC10 Philadelphia. (2024, March 7). Mother, boyfriend charged in death of missing 4-year-old Damari Carter. *NBC Philadelphia.*

https://www.nbcphiladelphia.com/news/local/damari-carter-philadelphia-duffel-bag-charges/3794046/

Philadelphia Police Department. (2024, March 6). *Update: Missing child investigation* [Press release].

https://www.phillypolice.com/news/update-missing-child-investigation-damari-carter/

Context & system references (used implicitly, not instructional)

Centers for Disease Control and Prevention. (2024). *About child abuse and neglect.*

https://www.cdc.gov/child-abuse-neglect/about/index.html

World Health Organization. (2024, November 5). *Child maltreatment.*

https://www.who.int/news-room/fact-sheets/detail/child-maltreatment

U.S. Department of Health and Human Services, Administration for Children and Families, Children's Bureau. (2025). *Child Maltreatment 2023.*

https://acf.gov/cb/report/child-maltreatment-2023

www.ingramcontent.com/pod-product-compliance
Ingram Content Group UK Ltd.
Pitfield, Milton Keynes, MK11 3LW, UK
UKHW020720110326
11196UKWH00015B/1339